Recipes from My Garden

Herbs and Memoir Short Prose and Poetry

Nadja Maril

Recipes from My Garden

Herbs and Memoir Short Prose and Poetry

ISBN: 978-1-957224-34-3 (paperback)
ISBN: 978-1-957224-35-0 (ebook)

Printed in the United States of America.

FIND US AT

oldscratchpress.com
currentwords.com

For Peter

CONTENTS

Foreword

March 2020, I worked on my novel, having just completed my MFA program, and my husband and I unpacked and arranged the furniture inside the historic house we'd been renovating for two-plus years. We reseeded the grass, rented a tent, and invited family and friends to celebrate our daughter's wedding scheduled for the end of the month.

And then the world shut down.

The dining table became our office and my husband, Peter, and I broke up our days by taking long walks with our dog. We waved at neighbors from a distance, afraid of the virus.

At night I worried about the health of my three children, one who lives 10,000 miles away, and their families. To calm my mind, I put together sentences to describe past memories and this seemed to help me achieve some sleep. In my kitchen I revisited old recipes and tried out new ones. Peter planted the first of several vegetable gardens on the hill where Alex and Josh were to exchange their wedding vows. I added herb plants in between the flowers.

The prose and poetry in the pages that follow were primarily written between April 2020 and December 2023.

Sunflowers (2)

In front of our house, I see a row of smiling faces. Hidden in the velvet gold centers of our sunflowers, eyes and smiles peer back at me. Future seeds to be stolen by squirrels, fringed by yellow petals, they encircle the perimeter of the garden. Tourists snap photographs. Neighbors wait for them to appear. Seasonally, we are the sunflower house.

Inside my house hangs a sunflower painting by my father, oil paint on canvas. One single flower on a bare stem surrounded by tufts of grass, it leans on a split rail fence of mismatched rectangles. Triangle petals around a dark orange circle. His vision. White sheets hang on a clothesline and I imagine them waiting to be lifted by the wind, fragrant with the smells of earth and sky.

I visit the images of other artists and study their sunflowers. Soft and round. Pale and luminous. Each sees the world differently. I savor the difference. And I remember my sunflowers and their welcoming gaze.

Recipes from My Garden

Herbs and Memoir Short Prose and Poetry

HERBS and RECIPES

Cilantro

We plant the seeds and wait for Chinese parsley to erupt from the earth. I keep checking the brown patch of soil daily. Nothing. And then, just two tiny bits of green. By the end of the week, delicate leaves and stems sway in the breeze. The name may change--Mexican parsley, Chinese parsley, Coriandrum sativum, cilantro— but the herb is the same. Once the plants are thick and strong, I crush them in my hand to smell their scent.

This is my little bit of earth. A place of possibilities where ingredients are created.

One quarter of all humans think cilantro tastes like soap, but I am not among them. On my tongue the flavor is exotic. Tart. I add the chopped leaves to stir amongst fried vegetables seasoned with soy and ginger, grateful to experience the highs and lows of this summer herb. So much of life is out of my control, but in the kitchen I'm mistress and master.

I heap a bouquet on top of grilled fish and imagine sitting in a brightly tiled courtyard, sun on my back as I dip corn chips into salsa and guacamole seasoned with vibrant cilantro. In this place, this moment, I taste the universe.

Tomato Harvest Management

I slice into asymmetrical curves of tender flesh for sandwiches, gazpacho, and salads. Our tomatoes taste sweet but possess thick white cores. Amateur gardeners. We feast.

The young plants purchased, planted, and placed inside wire cages grow tall and dense with leaves so thick, within their shadows tomato fruit hides. I spend a few minutes each morning crouching on the ground looking upwards. Investigating. I see a gaping bite. A wild creature has sampled our crop by moonlight. Savored the tart juice of a barely ripe tomato.

Time to mix cornmeal and spices. Time to fry green tomatoes.

Sunflowers

Through my kitchen window I see the sunflowers you planted. A tangle of green leaves, stalks, and soft velvet gold competing for the earth. An assembly of witnesses to a passing parade of joggers, pedestrians, baby strollers and dogs on leashes. They stand sentry to protect what you've left behind.

Admiration for My Grandmother's Pitcher

Blooming flowers and interlocking leaves encircle the belly of my grandmother's silver pitcher. The French word for this hammering technique which creates a textural surface, repousse, literally translates as pushback.

Repousse. Pushback, I like the concept of pushing outwards to stand one's ground. I think of push-ups. Opposing gravity. The act of asserting oneself to create something new. The garden shapes on the pitcher's midsection are yielding yet firm.

I look at the pitcher and recall Sunday dinners: chicken fricassee, green beans, grandmother's special noodles—wide ones on the bottom and crisp fried skinny noodles on top —plus coleslaw. Traveling back in time to when I was eight years old, I tread down the long dark hallway lined with odd chairs to the pantry where I'd watch my grandmother add a large spoonful of mayonnaise, a small spoonful of sour cream and a few drops of French dressing to the grated cabbage and carrot. In the kitchen, she'd prepare the chicken, fresh from the farmers market. Generously sprinkle salt and pepper and Kitchen Bouquet to turn the skin a warm brown in the oven.

The front room of the Baltimore row house where my mother grew up was referred to as "the parlor." The formality of the word matched its contents, upholstered chairs protected by dustcovers I watched being made from scraps of floral fabric on the treadle sewing machine. Carpets with bright geometric patterns covered the dark wood floors where I'd line up my dominoes to strategically fall, while my mother and grandmother sat on the stiff couch, their reedy voices rising and falling.

At dinnertime the round table in the center of the house was laden with dishes: warm dinner rolls, stewed fruit, green beans flavored with bacon, and the silver pitcher. I remember the time my grandmother made potato kugel in a cast iron corn stick pan, because my dad's favorite part of the kugel were the crispy brown edges. Dad laughed at the tiny helpings of kugel shaped like miniature ears of corn. We'd eat until we were more than full, and Grandmother would insist on making chicken sandwiches for me and my brother's school lunches.

I was taught to appreciate fine things at a young age. Small transportable items, things of value you can take when you're on the run. My great-grandfather, who repaired watches and jewelry, fled a Russian shtetl with his wife and two babies to escape anti-Semitic persecution. Gold and silver trinkets probably helped pay their passage.

I like to think this pitcher is a family heirloom. Owned by one of my great-grandmothers Bertha or Sadie, but it could have just as easily been someone else's cast-off. Grandmother sometimes had an entire rack of coats, clothes she'd collect to re-distribute to the needy. Stacks of chocolate bars, playing cards and dominoes awaited shipment to military bases overseas in the spare room, while shirt boxes filled with odd pieces of jewelry became craft projects for bedridden patients. One friend, the widow of a sea captain, gave grandmother most of her belongings, because her second husband wanted nothing of the first husband in the house. Nothing to remember him by, but perhaps when she visited my grandmother she could see them still. Very fine things, Chinese cloisonné and an ebony table with elephant tusks.

After she inherited the silver pitcher, my mother continued to prefer her pottery one for serving guests. It was more her style. She worried about the valuables in our house and when we left for long trips, she used to hide the silver pitcher in the clothes hamper underneath dirty towels.

Acquiring quality used items is a skill I mastered. Buying and selling antiques helped pay the bills. I took pride in setting up beautiful displays and learning the provenance of each piece. Packing and unpacking each item carefully, so nothing would break. I toted heavy boxes. Conveying history.

Possession or admiration of artistry? I've broken the habit. How much does one person or one family need and use? It's what the objects cause me to think about, that draws me to them. The stories they tell me the longer I gaze.

Some items I craved in my twenties, the ornate set of silver my mother refused to relinquish, no longer seems attractive to me decades later. Owning things that are valuable, easily stolen and pawned, requires care and responsibility. I can find simpler things that are easier to throw away.

Pushback, a refusal to follow in the footsteps of my predecessors. Do without something long enough and you realize you never needed it. The status items important to someone else are not necessarily important to you.

I keep the silver pitcher inside the corner cupboard, behind glass doors. In places where the plating has grown thin, glints of copper warm the patina. My grandmother filled this pitcher with iced tea for company. She brewed the black tea extra strong and added water and ice. We added lemon and sugar.

The Nature of Basil

I pluck four thick green leaves and inhale the aromatic scent. How do I describe the smell? Fresh. Almost mint. Aromatic.

I recall my first introduction to fresh herbs. Eight years old, seated between adults, the familiar smell of tomato sauce wafts across the table. The artist chef is excited to serve us each a small yellow bowl of something he wants us to share.

"Simple," he says, "So simple but so delicious." Spaghetti marinara topped with a few pieces of fresh picked basil.

I point my nose toward the green leaves in the middle and sniff. Yes. This is something new. The noodles are thick. Cooked al dente. The sauce clings to their edges. Eat until satiated.

I listen to stories told while wine is sipped from jelly glasses. Study the wrinkles on the old people's faces and hear their laughter.

Basil is no longer something dried and sprinkled from a bottle. Faded green dust. These leaves are bright and moist. Young. I place one on my tongue and taste summer.

Red Tomato Harvest

I search for shiny red amongst the chaos of green
Leaves and vines tangled within our once tidy garden
Miraculously produce fruit not seen last night.
As if by instantaneous regeneration,
Tomatoes: scarlet, orange, crimson
Beauteous red orbs, full and ripe, again fill my baskets.

Hidden when green, now visible when red.
A reverse game of red light, green light.
I kneel in the earth looking upwards
Pluck and pull, tug and twist to the right
Gathering my bounty for a stew.

My hands stinging from their acid
I remove seeds and skins to reveal
Pink juices. Carmine flesh. Colors bright inside.
My reward: white soup bowls filled with Gazpacho
Tomato soup, red sauce
Salsa, tomato pie.
Comfort food, the red joy of tomatoes
Resides in my belly and I am satisfied.

Fall Garden

A web of miniature tributaries cover the tough skin of the orange tap root I've seized from the soil. Earth clinging to its surface, the smell ignites memories of savory stews and crunchy salads. Sweet when roasted and satisfying when raw. Peter Rabbit, did he ever dig up a carrot or did he judiciously nibble on the feathery green tops? Carrot top pesto. A cousin in taste to parsley, I add the leaves to salads, sauces and stews. Root vegetables prosper in the cold. I don a wool sweater and kneel on the damp ground surveying our riches.

Rosemary

While other herbs wither and freeze in the cold, rosemary endures the snow. A bit of green on a dreary day. Just a six-inch branch can add fragrance to a miniature flower arrangement in January.

I bend to break off a stem to inhale the scent, but for harvesting recommend sharp scissors because the stalks are thick. Hearty and pliable, they bend and shape themselves to the will of the wind, making them not at all like the perfect upside-down cones, miniature Christmas trees, sold during the holidays. I used to purchase one for the table before we planted an herb garden. They never lasted longer than a few weeks. I hate to waste anything, so I began to search for ways to use all that dried rosemary in breads, salads, and beverages. Did you know that rosemary tea makes an excellent hair rinse thought to add shine and promote growth? The excess I'd tie to a rafter in the basement with a ribbon and a plan to add it to homemade sachets, which I never did because cooking with rosemary is what I like best.

Tucked inside pockets my knife creates in the leg of lamb or slid underneath the roasting chicken's skin, the smell of rosemary wafting from the oven comforts me with its earthy scent. I pull the needle-shaped leaves off the plant's stems, twist and crush them between my fingers and add a bit of rosemary to a bread stuffing. Cooking in summer on the grill or in winter in the kitchen, rosemary smells delicious. It's something I want to share.

Gardeners Call Them Volunteers

Spring lettuce, tender green ruffles against a backdrop of brown soil.
A gift from the previous season.
Sprouted from seeds that slept through the winter.
I wait for the lettuce heads to grow round and full.

I think of the crinolines I wore beneath my skirt as a child
To feel beautiful
Listening to the swish of crunching lace, starched layers of fabric,
Elastic encircling my waist.
Each head of lettuce an upside-down petticoat
A field of green petticoats
Rustling as the wind blows.

Leaves of curly lettuce
Nestled in the bottom of the salad bowl
Encircling the radishes, carrots, and tomatoes.
A drizzle of olive oil and malt vinegar
Tossed with cucumber slices and parsley.
I gather what I can on a fork
Grateful for my finery.

Love and the Kitchen

I remember from childhood a special sausage wrapped up in a sheet of white butcher paper my grandmother would buy for us at the city farmers' market.

Plump and pink, we cooked the links in a small tightly covered frying pan until the grease they created began to sizzle and pop. So different from the skinny little sausages in cardboard packages from the supermarket, I wondered how they could share the same name. The sausages were ready when the outsides were crusty and brown and the insides white and tan.

Jews were not supposed to eat pork, but my mother's family reinterpreted the rules. Her grandmother born in Nashville, Tennessee, in deference to kosher laws didn't serve bacon or sausage on the Sabbath that started at sundown on Friday and ended on sundown on Saturday, a day of rest and prayer observed by all devout Jews. But on other days of the week she served whatever was in season. Her menus included glazed ham, pan fried pork chops, country sausages and Smithfield bacon alongside fresh asparagus and hand-made noodles that were said to be legendary. Traditional favorites like potato *latkes* and *tzimme*s made with carrots, sweet potato, prunes and brisket were served alongside dishes of mashed turnips, fried chicken and catfish. She made an angel food cake, it was told to me during childhood, so light and airy it would float off the table.

"How is that possible?" I'd ask.
"You had to be there," Mother and Grandmother would say.

My father's parents came to the United States from Lithuania as teenagers. Strict Orthodox Jews, they kept a kosher household. No meat was consumed with dairy. No shellfish. No pork and no bending of the rules.

Father was the youngest of six children. Butter could not be on the same table with meat. For a special treat, his mother would give him schmaltz (chicken fat) spread on rye bread. Food was precious.

When my parents got married, my father was the one who knew how to cook. He taught my mother how to make a meat loaf smothered with onions and surrounded by slices of zucchini, carrots and mushrooms.

My mother elaborated on my father's meatloaf recipe and invested in several cookbooks including *The Joy of Cooking*. She became proficient at making split pea soup, lentil soup, and chicken soup with matzo balls. Starting with the basics, she kept adding new dishes.

I remember the first night she proudly brought a roasted pork shoulder seasoned with garlic and fennel to the dinner table. A crisp brown sheath of fat encircled the moist fragrant meat. Oven browned potatoes surrounding the roast luxuriated in the drippings. On the side were baked apples stuffed with raisins.

My father, remembering the kosher laws of his childhood, asked "What kind of meat is this?"

"It's good meat," my mother answered. "Trust me." He ate the pork reluctantly, because my mother served it. Such is love.

Parsley

Karpas, a raw green vegetable
Leafy and bright
The Hebrew word for the green herb on our Seder plate
Parsley from my garden
To witness this holy night of remembering.

We pass around a sprig to dip in saltwater before eating
A table ritual for everyone
Our food dipped in tears.
The salt and garden plant on my tongue
I remember everyone who's ever been enslaved
Around the world
And here in my own nation
Where there are those who would have us remember nothing.

Green, the color of new beginnings
Parsley, a mild tasting herb
I think of parslied potatoes, parsley rice, parsley in my tuna fish,
Chopped up in my eggs
The Karpas on the plate represents what Jewish people
Ate in Egypt when enslaved.
Poor people's food.

Parsley, in my garden it survives winter
Undaunted by the cold, it continues to grow
Tall and thick, stem stiff and crunchy
I crop the offshoots
Assembling a bouquet of hardy green leaves.

Green, the parsley is bright green
Green, conserving our dwindling resources
Green, caring about what we use and eat
So many different meanings for something so basic
As the color of vegetables processing sun's energy
Used as a garnish on dinner plates
Strong and sturdy, in adverse circumstances
A reminder, to be kind to one another.

Cucumbers

Pleasant, bland and refreshing
The unassuming cucumber
Dressed in pepper, salt, and vinegar
Takes on a new persona.

Dense flesh easily chilled
Crisp when sliced
Slathered in creamy yogurt and dill
Pickled in brine or grilled
I look for ways to use the unexpected
Surplus of weighty green submarines
Invading our hill of uncut grass.

In our garden our cucumbers
Are anything but elegant
Hidden and forgotten
Beneath tangles of leaf and vine
On the verge of turning yellow
We remember them
Stretching fingers through weeds
Feeling for their thick skin
An armor against insect invaders.
No protection from neglect.

Ashamed I search for recipes
Not wanting these dear vegetables
To go to waste when food is precious.
They enhance tabouli salad, gazpacho,
Chevre and watercress sandwiches.
Excellent with avocadoes and radishes
My favorite discovery, to serve them grilled
Beneath a savory sauce of tomatoes and cilantro
Topped with mozzarella cheese
Reminding me it is never too late to redeem
What is almost lost and can be shared.
I serve them at a dinner party.
Taste my excellent cucumbers, I say.
Grown in our own garden.
Fresh picked today.

Recipe for Fried Tofu

Buy extra firm and check the expiration date
Cut into one-inch cubes and set upon a plate
Dusted with baking soda, sprinkle more on top
Heat oil in a frying pan until you hear it pop.

I use sesame and olive oil, not too much
When adding the tofu cubes don't let them touch
Wait until each side turns a crisp golden brown
Patiently, before flipping sideways and down.

Once complete, place on paper towels to drain
Diagonally slice vegetables to make this your main
Meal of the day, remember favorite Chinese dishes
Breaking open fortune cookies, reading wishes
Soy sauce, oyster sauce, hot mustard, all comfort food
Sweet and sour tang puts you in a better mood.

Add scallions, mushrooms, carrots, snow peas,
Whatever you find in the crisper drawer will please.
But do not forget the garlic, plus ginger is good
Zucchini, string beans, asparagus, if a vegetable could
Sauté well, use it, then mix in your favorite sauce
To this, you one by one, add fried tofu and gently toss.

Serve with noodles, lettuce, or rice
A side of sliced tomatoes or avocado is nice.
Crown with fresh herbs: cilantro, basil, parsley, mint
Compliments will follow. No need to hint.

The Simple Joys of Baking Cake

I taught myself to bake during childhood. First it was the store-bought brownie mix. Add water and eggs. Then it was the discovery of sweet icing spread between layers of moist cake. The smooth stripe of glossy chocolate within each triangle slice.

The photo accompanying the magazine recipe for Lady Baltimore Cake seduced me. I crooned as I gathered the ingredients. Begin with yellow cake mix, add grated orange peel, real butter and six eggs. Cover with a sweet and sour orange juice glaze and decorate with candied tangerine segments.

Too beautiful to cut, my parents said, but eat it we must. Shared with guests, I bask in the glory of my accomplishment.

Years later, I look for the recipe. The name I remember is associated with an entirely different dessert. Figs, raisins and pecans divide layers of sponge cake lavishly covered with vanilla cream frosting first said to be served in the city of Charleston.

I create my own dessert. A fusion of old and new. Candied pecans plus oranges. Tart red cranberries replace the raisins. Powdery substances mixed into liquid when heated still create a miracle. The sweet bread of life we call cake.

My Recipe for Chicken and Rice

Have you ever tried my chicken baked with onions and rice?
A cold weather dish to warm you up, it's really quite nice.

Start with chicken pieces, quartered by yourself to save money.
Place in a deep casserole with broth and add a little honey
Fresh chopped basil, two large onions, pepper and salt.
Bake two hours on simmer, achieving comfort to exult.

A ratio of one to two, broth to raw rice, thirty minutes before serving
Forget take-out delivery, a homecooked meal you are deserving.
Accompany with crisp greens, sliced cucumber, tomatoes bright red
Your salad ingredients must be fresh and ripe, I've always said.

Hurray for the dinner that makes you feel warm inside
Share with those you love. Soul nutrition it will provide!

Menudo

We used to play a silly game one summer when I was twelve years old. My friend Leslie and her younger sister Wendy and I would concoct strange food combinations and then dare one another to taste our creation— blindfolded. We'd mix odd things like peanut butter and ham. Peppered ice cream. Some of our experiments tasted good.

I've tried all sorts of odd things in my life. Octopus. Fermented herring. Kidney pie. More than once I had Campbell's Pepper Pot Soup made with tripe. So when you suggested Menudo, the ingredients didn't bother me. I jumped at the chance to taste something new.

Menudo, a traditional Mexican stew, known to be a curative for hangovers. Tripe and hominy in a red chili broth. Optional garnishes: raw onion, dried oregano, wedges of lime, fresh chili. Comfort food consumed with warm tortillas on a Sunday before noon.

Young, I think I can tame a wolf. Enchant you into remaining my faithful companion. I savor our hot passion. Ignore broken dates. Other lovers. I want to believe your excuses. Endure the bite and sting on my tongue and wait for sweetness that never arrives.

Re-imagining our time together I see you, faded shades of mahogany and gold, words soft and mushy like the hominy in my stew.

Nostalgic for the aroma of you, I go to the market and return with the needed ingredients for Menudo. The tripe's honeycomb surface, shiny white, fascinates me. I cut the cow's stomach into small pieces and admire the maze of tiny chambers. Into the pot I toss the marrow bone, cow's feet, garlic, onion, and tomato to simmer.

Surrounded by cooking smells, I discover pleasure in self-reliance.

NATURE and NURTURE

We Bought the Kelly Green Dress

Mother and I roam department stores looking for bargains. We hover over tables of marked-down sweaters in the Girl's Department. Ponder the merits of silk and sequined cocktail attire in Lady's Better Dresses. As her assistant in the dressing room, I inhale the L'Aimant perfume on her discarded tan sweater as she steps out of her tweed skirt.

"How do I look?" she asks while adjusting the matching satin jacket and chiffon scarf that encircles her neck to complete the ensemble. The emerald shade compliments the gold highlights in her hair.

It's as if we've stepped into a fairytale. "You look glamorous," I say. "You have to buy it."

We are co-conspirators as she reaches in her purse for her credit card. Elated at our purchase we celebrate with ice cream at the soda counter. Hum and hold hands crossing the parking lot to the car.

Sorting through Mother's things, a month after her death, I find the dress hanging in the back of her closet and press it close to my face. A trace of scent remains. The fabric caresses my skin. I imagine wearing it while kicking my legs high as I dance. Perhaps with some alterations, it could be my new party dress. The tailor attempts with straight pins to re-configure the size 16 garment to my slender shape. A futile exercise.

The way to remember my mother is to buy a new dress. I will imagine her with me in the dressing room when I decide which one fits me best. In her honor I will treat myself to something extravagant.

At Age Eight We Were Young Enough to Trespass

The grass came up to our waists.
Bare armed, we swam through dandelions and choke weed
Ignoring welts and scratches.
To stand before two wise giants.

Clothed in gray bark
Possessing wide trunks.
One limb on each, bent upward at the elbow.
The other branches growing towards the sky.

They beckoned us to climb and hang.
Enchanted, we straddled the branches and played.
Feet dangling above the earth.
Mosquitoes buzzing in our ears.

Until our mouths became dry and we remembered the raspberries,
Growing somewhere along the fence.
Guarded by poison ivy and thorny shrubs
Hidden among scratchy leaves
Each seed encased in deep rose flesh.
A delicate construction of orbs.
Connected but independent.
Tiny sweet gems.

I saw the raspberries as little houses,
Topping the end of each prickly stem.
Fairy food.
Hidden on this property where no one lived
Discovered by a few stray children.
Miraculous how they dissolved so quickly on our tongues.

Freedom

Christine's backyard has ducks and a brown muddy pond where the grass refuses to grow. She is two years older than me and I'm in awe of her long orange hair. She knows things that kindergarteners don't know. She shows me where her brother and father pee behind the garage and where her father hides his shotgun.

Giddy with independence, I don't tell my parents I am leaving Christine's house or where to find me. Wearing her sister's purse and sunhat, we are searching for new lands. We are on an adventure like in Winnie the Pooh's *expotition* to the North Pole.

Skipping down the hill we arrive at a big house with brown flaking paint and wide front porch. No one is living here. After chasing each other around the yard, we settle atop the wood swings hanging from thick ropes. The air smells of fresh cut wood and autumn leaves.

The creaking of the swings fills my ears, muffling the sound of footsteps.

Smack. Father's hand slaps my bottom. The pain is sharp and swift.

Surprise brings tears to my eyes. Shamed, I refuse to cry.
Christine will think me babyish. I turn away.

"Look at me," he hollers. "Mother and I have been looking everywhere. Do you know how worried we were? Do you have any idea?"

Stunned, I retreat into the piece of time just minutes earlier—pumping my legs with the wind swooshing past my face. Excited to make a new friend. An explorer expanding my territory. I have no words with which to answer. My first taste of freedom and I have no regrets.

Voice Lessons

Back and forth, I swing myself in our backyard. Small hands wrapped around metal chains. High sounds coming from my throat. An early memory.

"We've been listening to your daughter's singing," our neighbor Mrs. Clark says.

Mother looks at me and I look back at her confused. I stand very still and pretend to be invisible.

"Singing?" Mother repeats.

"Out on the swing, in your backyard," Mrs. Clark says. "Very high and sweet. Like an angel."

Singing? Is that what I'd been doing while pumping my legs as fast as they could go to lift my swing higher. The sound flew from my mouth. Behind closed eyelids, colors danced. Whoosh. The metal swing set continued to creak as I flew effortlessly up towards the stars.

Traveling through the heavens on my swing, the three-year-old me was invincible. No need for companions or words, just melodies. I hadn't thought about what I was doing, until Mrs. Clark gave it a name.

I listen to my parents' recordings of Harry Belafonte singing "Day-O" and sing along. Fashioning a make-believe microphone for myself from the gold painted cylinder piece on a cord that raised and lowered the lamp in the corner, I stand beside my father's easy chair and perform for an imaginary audience.

One day my parents play a Joan Baez record. What a beautiful voice. Her nose is even a little crooked like my own. I learn all her songs. A guitar is given to me for my 11th birthday and I wait for lessons that summer.

In fifth grade music, our entire class of 30 children sing "Swing Low, Sweet Chariot," rehearsing to perform it for a school assembly.
"Would anyone like to sing a verse alone?" the teacher asks.
I raise my hand.

"Yes, give it a try," she says. I sing a verse, and she assigns me both verses.

"Do you take voice lessons?" my classmates ask afterwards. "You sound like an opera singer."

Can someone teach you how to sing? Wasn't singing something you just did, matching your voice to the notes played on the piano?

Always the last to be picked for the softball or soccer team, I'm the girl who wears odd clothes and talks differently. Are they actually complimenting me? I can't wait to get home to share my good news.

* * *

Not everyone likes my high voice. That's okay. I can make music. Any kind I want. My voice is my instrument.

Mrs. Lacey, my voice teacher in college, has long dark hair and a complexion that makes me think of rosy cheeked children playing in the snow. She tells me she is looking for "pure sound."

During my weekly private lesson, she talks about her baritone husband's career. "It's so much easier for him to find work," she says. "There's an excess of sopranos."

She takes apart each phrase I sing to find my flaws. "It's all about the breath," she says, "like sipping through a straw. You are the vessel that creates sound."

My pronunciation of Italian, German, French needs correction. My vowel sounds should be more open. In our group classes, it is the other students who she praises. I keep practicing and hear only criticism. I begin to doubt whether I should be singing.

During second semester I audition for sophomore chorus. Alone on the wooden stage, I remind myself to stand tall with shoulders relaxed. Breathing through my nose as I was taught, I struggle to inhale. My knees are shaking and my voice is trembling. Twice the choir director asks me if I am really majoring in voice. Ashamed, I stare at the floor.

I transfer to another university. Change my major to anthropology and begin to sing only for myself – while washing dishes, driving, or in the shower accompanied by the patter of water against my back.

Gradually, I lose myself in my singing and stop worrying if anyone is listening. The keening sound of high notes vibrating in my cheekbones gives me comfort, expressing joy and sadness. So maybe I am not meant to be a performer, at least not a classical one. I pull out my guitar and make up my own songs. Or sing old favorites and pick and strum – varying the timing and the rhythm.

Several decades later, married and with children in school, I join a choir. It feels good to sing in a group. As long as I sing the right notes, no one is judging me. When asked to sing a small solo, I still feel nervous remembering my previous failures.

Members of the congregation greet me afterwards. "I didn't know you could sing. What a nice voice." A small triumph, to manage a line of music for an audience on my own. In my estimation, however, my performance is lacking.

I vocalize each day. Practice new and familiar melodies. Revisiting old territory, I sip in air until I feel my rib cage and back begin to expand. My goal is to reclaim what was lost. Feet firmly planted on the ground, more forgiving of myself for past mistakes, I relax into the melody and embrace the power of the vibrations. I can do this.

Projecting a loud steady tone conveys power and freedom. Not to be judged, but to be heard. My emotions shape themselves into sound. The wings inside my spirit open as the song reaches the sky. The freedom returns, the simple pleasure of a child singing on a swing.

The Land Holds My Memory

Somewhere there are photos, color slides taken in the late 1960's of me sitting on top of a large rock. Buck teeth, hair held back from my face with a kerchief, and scrawny legs. My parents have just purchased a piece of land. It is a nice lot, 7/8 of an acre in Truro, Massachusetts near the tip of Cape Cod.

Every July during my childhood we visit this land to pick blueberries. We could pick them near the dunes, but these are our blueberries. The lot began at the top of a hill and sloped downward towards wetland. A road marks the bottom perimeter. The rock, as tall as my father, sat on the opposite side. Prickly blackberry vines run along the edge of the marsh, weaving in and out amongst the poison ivy.

In the distance is Corn Hill, the famous spot where the Pilgrims in search of provisions found corn, the buried seed stock of the Nauset Indians, before sailing towards Plymouth. A plaque at the base of the hill tells the story of their "gift" of corn. The native population was decimated by the arrival of Europeans spreading disease.

My parents couldn't afford a view of the water, so they picked a lot facing the protected wetlands. From my perch on the rock I can look down on my parents' heads and in the opposite direction gaze clear across the marsh. I can see orange, gray and yellow birds in flight and the brown tips of cattails. The colors blend into a woven landscape of dark and light.

We pick the fat blackberries in August. Carefully I'd fill my pail, avoiding the shiny three leaves of green turning red. Wash my hands with harsh brown soap when I return home.

I have childhood memories of walks in the woods. The emergence of mushrooms after a rain, the fragrant smell of pine needles as I hunted for baby toads. My father made sketches of the house they planned to build, and I imagined waking up to the sounds of bird calls. His pencil drawings stayed in a drawer.

Meanwhile, the other neighbors built their houses. A previously blocked fire road brought more traffic. Large lots got subdivided. Hardtop replaced dirt roads. The resulting soil erosion changed the landscape.

The arriving Europeans who settled on Cape Cod came with plans to tame the wilderness. While many made their living as fishermen, there were also farmers. They chopped down trees to build houses and beneath their feet the sandy earth began to shift, creating the famous sand dunes. They had no idea how important the trees and native vegetation were to stabilizing the soil.

In 2007 my husband Peter and I started to build a house, and he explored the terrain across the road. The start of the wetlands is not where I remembered it from childhood, and I am disoriented by the changes. Inexplicably the large rock in my childhood photos had vanished.

The blackberries were gone, replaced with brush and hardwood. So many trees took root in the expanse still considered a marsh, the view I remember had been erased. But across the land wild things still grew; cranberries, blueberries, scrub pines, pokeberry, golden rod, and thistles. I looked for the gullies where I remembered the vines.

Soil erosion from the houses built during the past fifty years, roads and traffic has changed the landscape. It since filled in wetlands. I am the witness.

Although we tried to keep the landscape as natural as possible and plant native species— beach roses, bayberry, and daisies—in soil displaced by construction, just by our actions of building on the land we have already altered the environment once again.

By the time we finish the house our three children are too old to take for walks to hunt for toads, but they are able to use it for weekend getaways and a place to quarantine during the coronavirus pandemic. Perhaps one day we'll take our grandchildren to dig for quahogs at low tide and show them where rosehips can be gathered to brew delicious tea.

Change is inevitable. Sandbars move and cliffs of sand crumble. Beach shores erode as the winds shift and the sea level rises. Soil has seeped into many of the Cape Cod marshes. I remind myself to embrace the unexpected as I age. Adapt.

Deer still hide in the Truro wetlands. I spy them while walking at sunrise and at dusk. I hear coyotes at night. When the trees are bare, from my deck as the sun lowers itself in late afternoon, the light reflected off the cattails and tall grasses shimmers with warm, gold hues. While breakfasting I hear the twittering, hooting and calling of multiple birds and see flocks of wild turkeys rambling over the land.

"Isn't this the rock you keep talking about?" Peter says.

"How did it get there?" I ask. The boulder Peter finds is set back ten feet from the road. If he helps me to keep my balance to gain a foothold, I can hoist myself up and once again I sit and look out across the waving reeds towards Corn Hill.

Hidden behind tall trees and bushes, the large rock I remember from childhood never moved. The world around it changed.

Bareback Rider

The painting on the easel is taller than me. I am four years old in my father's studio located in the garage behind our house. I look at the woman standing on the back of a white horse. The horse is being led by a man holding two yellow balloons. The balloons are almost invisible, translucent like two soap bubbles. Is one of them meant for me?

The dancer, for she must be one to balance herself as the horse is walking, wears a tutu. She and the skirt defy gravity. I am captivated.

To someone else, the woman may appear abstract, without a face, hair, or detail. But I like this sort of figure because it allows me to fill in everything that has been erased and make her into whoever I want. This absence gives power to my child's mind. The world is full of possibilities and I fill in the blanks. I want to be a dancer. I want to twirl and point my toes, holding one leg high behind me in an arabesque.

"I like your painting. The lady on the white horse."

"Do you?"

I feel important. It's just me and my dad. I have him all to myself.

I see the familiar array of wood stretchers and rolls of canvas in one corner and a worktable with two drawers below and a slab of marble where my father mixes his paints. The studio smells familiar. The scent of oil paints and turpentine remind me of the aroma of my father's plaid shirts and khaki pants.

The circus? I think but do not ask. I've never been to a circus but I've seen pictures on the curtains in my room. The bright colors of circus tents; red, green, and blue. Always there are beautiful horses and bareback riders wearing tiaras and feathers in their hair and a ringmaster with top hat and boots.

It is an exotic world. Wild animals. Elephants. Perhaps I've seen this world on our black and white TV or on the pages of a picture book. My father lifts me up, hugs me to him. He smells of coffee and tobacco. I'm still small enough to balance on his shoulders, a wonderful way to make the journey back to our house.

The painting is finished. Exhibited. Stored in the racks of my father's studio, a larger studio. And maybe because it is one of the first paintings I remember consciously examining and discussing with my father, it sticks in my mind. Every so often I ask my mother or my father about that painting of the bareback rider, you know, the one with the white horse with a dancer on the horse's back. It's got red in it, a brilliant rectangle of red. My favorite color at age four. A vibrant hue that says look at me, look at me. I want to own that painting.

Years later it is mine. A housewarming gift when I moved into my first house. The title of this painting, "Vanishing Scene" is now an appropriate name. Circuses are past tense. Endangered species can no longer be caged. Horses must be treated with respect.

I stare at the painting and see the white steed is looking down. Reluctantly he follows the man dressed in blue. My eyes focus on the dancer with the long bare legs. She is me and I am her, performing for the audience. Secure and self-possessed. Not afraid of falling. Keeping her balance she remembers early childhood. She remembers watching her father devote time to his art. She remembers watching him paint in his studio. The two of them talking about a painting, this painting. Sharing a moment.

September's Catch

Dusk, we walk on the ocean's edge. Salt air in my nostrils. Dunes to my left and the crash of waves to my right for as far as I can see. I turn my head and see the slick head of a seal emerge for air and disappear into the surf. Four men stand at the water's edge fishing.

The seal is close to shore and I watch the shiny black head submerge itself and reappear several yards down the coastline as we walk. Our dog Chloe runs ahead to chase the ball. She's old in dog years, but at the beach she is full of energy. My husband Peter uses a long-handled thrower to hurl a ball that whistles above the sand. She never tires of this game.

The seals follow the fish. The sharks follow the seals. The fishermen complain. A few times Peter and I have cast our large poles into the ocean at high tide, but never caught anything. We suspect the seals devour the fish before they near land.

This group appears optimistic. I see a firepit dug into the sand. Sticks of wood ready to be lit. Two coolers.

I watch one cast out his line and hear his shout. His fist is raised. "I've got one," he says before reeling in his catch. We walk towards them to see the glint of silver scales. A striped bass twitching on the wet sand. They are young men, at least ten years younger than me.

The men look at us and likely see us as seniors. We have time to take long walks on the beach. But I feel vigorous in my stride. I can walk for miles on a night like this.

He pulls out his ruler. "Too small," he says and I feel his disappointment.

Chloe is anxious for another ball throw. Peter rewards her patience with a treat. She chases the ball and then rolls in the sand. A Cape Cod beach is her favorite place and she is reveling in the smells and textures.

Another moment and another shout. "I've got one." We run to get a glimpse of their catch. Again, the fish is measured as too small.

I imagine how delicious striped bass will be if immediately cleaned and thrown on the grill, consumed under the stars. The meat will be moist and fresh, served with just a touch of olive oil, lemon and salt. I've eaten such a feast, but never cooked on the beach.

A flashlight shines on the water as another bass is landed and measured. The dusk shifts into night. I reach for Peter's hand.

"It's a keeper!" the third man shouts. The man standing nearest to him, plants his rod deep in the sand and slaps him on the back. The other two call out their congratulations.

A rush of happiness surges through me. So many fish are running in this time and place, the seal and the men will have their dinners. And for one moment, with no fishing rod or bait, I am one of these fishermen.

Taking a Dip at Corn Hill

Delicious, is how I describe swimming this time of year.
The cold water, with the hot sun beating on my skin
Is easy to slip into, easy to glide through. Kick, Kick.
Splash, splash. The movement of my legs, my feet pliant paddles.
My arms, each one a windmill turning round and round.
And I imagine a gristmill. The wheel turns. The water flows
And ever so gently
Wheat is pummeled and ground.
I am limp and relaxed, floating
On my back, straight and pale.
So buoyant, I look up at the sky
And let the breeze carry me.
Until I remember my limbs
Start to kick my legs and I'm moving in a straight line
Or like a lazy frog, legs bent and then straight as if to hop,
Open and close. Kick and splash.
Lulled by the rhythm until I tire
Flip and dive to explore green shadows.

The Story of the Family Samovar

My great grandmother's samovar is made of brass, and for many years it sat on the top of a small marble top bureau in the hallway collecting dust. There's a little spout you turn where the water is supposed to come out and there's a tray underneath. It was used to heat hot water for tea. Hot coals were placed in the bottom. I imagine my ancestors huddled in a small thatched cottage, residing in a village in Ukraine where Jews were allowed to live. Shivering from the cold, they drink their strong hot tea in glass cups, wrapping their hands around the cups to stay warm. Too frightened to walk freely at night, worried the Cossacks may ride by on their broad horses swinging their swords, ready to indiscriminately beat up and rob any Jew foolish enough to show his face, they huddle around the samovar, study the Torah and tell stories.

During childhood I heard the stories about the shtetls and the pogroms that escalated to become the Holocaust where six million Jews—two-thirds of the Jewish population in Europe— were killed for no other reason than for being Jewish.

When my ancestors came to the United States, they brought their worldly possessions. The most valuable item was their samovar.

* * *

In my entire life, I have never seen the samovar used for any purpose. It is large and squat in shape. It moved from my grandmother's house to my mother's house after my grandmother died. The brass has grown dark and tarnished.

My daughter is getting married. She is dubious about wanting ownership of the samovar. She lives in a small apartment in northern California. She shares the results of her genetic profile with me. "I am fifty percent Ashkenazi," she says, "which means you are one hundred percent."

One hundred percent! I am surprised at the purity of my genetic heritage. But that is what the report from 23 and Me says. No mention of countries of origin. The gene pool from which I descend is so small that countries don't matter.

53

* * *

Ashkenazi, I like the way the four syllables sound, soothing and rhythmic on my tongue. Ashkenazi—a small tribe of Jews who moved into northern Europe, then migrated east, looking for a place to call home.
Americans of Christian heritage may find it exotic to discover they are ten or fifteen percent Ashkenazi, but the ratio doesn't work the other way. No outsiders ever joined the Ashkenazi community. The bloodline, my bloodline is pure.

* * *

"Are you Jewish?" I am my daughter's age, mid-twenties. At a cocktail party, an elderly woman from Albania asks me. "You have such a lovely complexion. Are you Jewish?" She stares at me and I hesitate. I look down at her wrinkled hands with glittering jewelry and try to think of what to say. I have never practiced the Jewish religion, never learned Hebrew, never was confirmed or had a bat mitzvah, but on the high holy days of Yom Kippur and Rosh Hashanah, I stayed home from school.

"Never forget you are Jewish," my father and mother would say. "It is your identity."

My fiancé has told me emphatically that if I do not practice the Jewish religion, I am not a Jew. He has rejected Catholicism and no longer considers himself a Catholic.

"It is a religion," he says. "Believe me. You are not Jewish."

"Are you Jewish?" the woman asks.

"No," I answer.

She smiles and compliments my dotted Swiss dress and my *fine young man*, before she starts to tell me about the filthy Jews who have stolen her waterfront property. "They have to be near the water because they stink and need to bathe all the time," she says. "They are all crooked lawyers, bankers, and thieves."

I am burning up inside and I want to tell her that Jewish people don't smell any different from anyone else or ask her why she would have to ask me if I am Jewish. I want to shake this elegant lady with her diamond earrings and her manicured nails and tell her she is the one who is dirty.

But I say nothing. I nod and act polite and rush outside to breath clean air as soon as our conversation has ended. I am angry. I am angry at myself. Ashamed that I'd let myself blend in with everyone else in the room instead of identifying myself as different. The next time someone asks me, I will answer, "Yes, that is my heritage."

My grandmother Pauline Schapiro told me stories about the farm where she grew up, the delicious sauerkraut they made and how she loved to eat the apples that fermented along with the cabbage. What she didn't tell me was how the children at school would make fun of her odd accent and how hard she worked to sound like everyone else. A fire in the courthouse provided the opportunity for Pauline and her sister Bessie to obtain replacement birth certificates saying they were born in America like their four younger siblings. She wanted to be able to proudly say she was an American.

The acts of discrimination are subtle. "He tried to Jew me down," a friend says describing an interaction at the local flea market.

"What did you say?"

My daughter Alex tells me that stress can affect your DNA, that centuries of persecution can cause molecular changes. I'm not certain that is true.

What I have observed is that we tend to create unreliable narratives about people different from ourselves when they remain strangers. The unfamiliar is scary.

I do not need my great grandmother's samovar to remind me of where I came from and who I am. I look in the mirror and see my high cheekbones and almond shaped eyes. In another decade, my hands will probably become as wrinkled as the hands that belonged to the lady from Albania. I carry the knowledge and tell the stories of those who lived before me. One of the *chosen people*—or maybe just one of many who have chosen to be proud of who we are.

Mint

You say let the mint grow wild. I say confine it to a pot.
Mint. I love it and I hate it.
Persistent invader, sprouting in improbable places
Almost choking out the small azalea bush
Encircling the lilies as they prepare to bloom
Pressing against the thriving parsley.
Troublemaker in the garden
Mint seizes every inch of available space.
I yank it up by the roots when you're not looking
And sneak it into the compost pile, underneath the coffee grounds.
But oh, it is delicious in my lamb stew.

The abundance of mint has challenged me to think of new ways to use it.
Before its tiny flowers have time to seed,
I add it to my flower arrangements.
The scent of mint freshens the room.
I put it in our ice water and on our morning fruit.
I add mint to peas and string beans and stuff it into spring rolls.
A necessity for mojitos and juleps
I dry mint branches for future tea.
But no matter how much mint I'm able to use,
Left unsupervised, it continues to grow and spread.

Tall stalks with oblong leaves
Rough texture on my tongue
I devour the green of its existence
And its resilience challenges me to embrace its strength.
I want to be like that mint
Never giving up, always seeking new territory
Revealing new flowers, even when trampled
Certain of myself and my progeny.

Back to School Night

I lift the turquoise and purple shawl out of the storage drawer and drape it over my shoulders. The caress of the soft yarn against my skin transports me to an earlier time and place.

I

I hear the clicking and buzz of insects through our backdoor screen as I put away the last of the dinner dishes. It feels like summer, but in Maryland our moist green surroundings are the norm for September and it's the beginning of a new school year for my two sons. I need to leave for *Back to School Night*. I get as far as the front hallway, cotton dress sticking to my shoulder blades, fiddling with my car keys, telling myself to open the front door.

My feet refuse to obey. I don't want to go. Please, a terrified voice inside me calls to my more rational self, do I have to go?

I picture the faces of the other parents, everyone staring at me. Or maybe it is the reverse, and I am the one staring at them. *Why is it that they get to have a life so normal they just assume tomorrow will be like yesterday?*

The other parents, like my neighbors, will try to avoid getting close enough for conversation. Even the lawyer who handled our house purchase quickly crossed the street, keeping his head down, when he saw me downtown. Why should tonight be any different?

Maybe he was crying. I know, it's sad. A nice family with young children moves to a small city to run their business, restoring antique lamps, and then one summer while they're back in Massachusetts, the husband dies of a stroke.

A single parent family is not what our foreign student, Giuliana, signed on for six months ago when we exchanged letters, but she has taken it in stride. An accomplished roller-skater and a sidewalk chalk artist, she is reading the boys the original version of *Pinocchio* one chapter a night. Nine months into her time with us, her father will commit suicide, forcing her home early. Perhaps the universe has chosen us intentionally, to show her a family living through trauma.

I start for the door until I remember my older son's first day of school a few days earlier. I replay the scene in my mind, standing alone awkwardly, snapping pictures with my husband's camera. Another mother complains to her friend, "My husband is always traveling. Always traveling. It's not fair." I struggle to maintain my composure. The woman's thoughtless words incite my heart to beat faster and faster.

I want to leave, but I stay and watch a little boy struggling to keep his new backpack square on his shoulders. The girl beside him is trying to loosen her braids. I imagine a kindly grandmother who must have pulled them too tight, striving for perfection. I sense the children's anticipation and their fear, and it moves through me like a wave. They are at the beginning of something that is both wonderful and frightening. Will they fit in with the others? Will they make a new friend?

I never fit in. Slightly different from the other girls in what I liked to do, in kindergarten I played Superman with two of the boys. We'd tie our nap blankets around our shoulders and run around the playground with our capes, pretending to fly.

As I grew older, I'd attempt to share some exciting news with one of the girls in elementary school, and they'd respond with a long drawn out *So?* Ashamed, I stared down at the floor. Boys seemed less judgmental.

"Step on their toe," was my Grandmother's advice. "Don't let them bother you," she said, "And then pretend it's an accident."

I will remember this advice at the Grief Workshop held at the Community College in October. The facilitator will tell us to think of all the people in our lives we've lost. Instead of thinking of my dead husband, I see my grandmother: blue eyes, fine pink skin, white crimped hair tinted blue, smelling like Lilies of the Valley. She never held back on taking action when required. My Grandmother told me she once paid a woman a dollar, in the days when one dollar was a lot of money, to stop playing the piano. *Was she really that bad?* I remember asking. Nothing frightened her. I will let nothing frighten me.

The retired podiatrist who lives across the street, greets me the week after my return to Annapolis with a question. "What are you going to do now?"

I struggle to make eye contact. "I'm going to keep going," I say. "Take care of my children."

Can people really be this obtuse? I replay the conversation repeatedly inside my mind. His lack of sensitivity seems to mirror eighty percent of the world. Each time I interact with someone new, I wonder on which side of the percentage chart they will fall.

II

I hold the smooth sharp car keys in jittery hands. Since I've returned to restart our life, I've avoided caffeine, but still the shakiness comes and goes and I've broken things. One of the casualties, a sweet lamp on my dressing table, pink and lavender flowers and butterflies painted on the inside of the frosted shade. I feel my dead husband's ghost watching me and shaking his head. What could I do? It didn't mean anything, I tell him. The world means nothing without you. My trembling hands got caught under the silk wrapped cord. The only thing worth saving is the silver-plated base.

I break the shower door a few days later. How does a thirty-five-year-old woman weighing 120 pounds manage to shatter a door of tempered glass? I recall the door being jammed and my struggling to close it before water got all over the floor. I remember staring at the nuggets of wavy glass covering the black and pink tiles, grabbing a towel and vacuum, embarrassed and concerned someone might get injured. That afternoon I buy a fabric shower curtain.

Sleep is intermittent. When I do sleep I have vivid dreams. In one dream, my dead husband is standing outside our house with the garbage cans, reminding me not to forget to put out the trash.

III

I'm standing in the hallway clasping the car keys, looking out our front window, when I see a strange car pulling into the driveway. *Probably this car wants to turn around.* But instead it stops and two people get out. I know them.

Karen is the mother of one of my younger son's friends. We've met a few times and arranged playdates, but she barely knows me. She and her husband were getting ready to attend *Back to School Night* and she thought of me.

She takes my hand and I feel my anxiety begin to fade.

"We thought it might be difficult for you tonight," she says, "and that it might be easier if you had some company. We'll drive you."

An angel. I am being visited by an angel. This angel has a broad face and strawberry blonde hair. Shorter and wider than me, she walks with determination. Karen is no stranger to loss. She has lost one breast, battling cancer. It has been replaced with surgery, but the replacement didn't take well, leaving ugly scar tissue. She understands how loss magnifies things. She tells me how loss makes life intense. Vividly beautiful is how she describes it.

When you are able to laugh, Karen tells me, you'll know you're starting to heal. Eventually I tell her about my neighbor, the retired podiatrist across the street.

IV

Karen and I become swimming buddies. Twice a week we swim laps while our children are in school, treating ourselves to a high calorie lunch or late breakfast afterwards. Karen, once a competitive swimmer, keeps track of her laps with pennies slipped from a small pouch at the end of her lane. I complete one lap for her three, a saltwater mermaid struggling to navigate the cement edges and chlorine of the County Pool, I wind my long hair inside a latex cap and wear swim googles. Always the googles are fogging up, but I'm gaining stamina. I appreciate the routine.

Because she owns her business, a children's consignment shop, she can make her own hours, so we dawdle over lunch, sharing life stories and aspirations for our futures. Eight months later it is to Karen I confide, "I think I met someone. His name is Peter and our first 'date' was at the County Pool swimming laps."

Another year passes and it is Karen who needs me. After six years of being cancer free, masses are detected in her liver and her lungs. An autologous bone marrow transplant might save her life. Whatever it takes, she tells me she will keep fighting. But just in case, we shop for children's books about loss and grief.

While waiting for the marrow transplant date, we pour over color charts and price shop her selections for new furniture. She plans a trip, a family cruise to Disney World and for her birthday that year I give her a handwoven shawl of turquoise and purple.

She meets Peter, but dies months before our wedding day. She never holds our baby girl born the following year. But when her husband returns the gift I gave her to have as a keepsake, I reluctantly accept it.

* * *

Comforted by the velvet texture of the soft yarn against my skin, I pull it closer. It's been a long time since shawls like this were in fashion. But I keep this one, to remember my friend.

Lost and Found

Missing, one gold earring.
Lost on a weeknight dinner date.
We retraced our walking route.
Inquired at the restaurant.
Nothing.
An unsolved mystery.

I blamed myself for being careless
Then told myself it's only an earring
And resigned myself to move on.

But my husband kept looking.
Three nights later, he saw it,
peeking out from a street crevice
As I strolled down the curving side street
Slightly ahead, enjoying the cold air on my face.
He called me back.

Bent down on one knee
He placed inside my palm
My earring,
battered but salvageable.
My hero.

We've shared our lives with one another
For thirty-one years.
Long enough to know nothing is ever perfect.
Dents and scars are okay with me.

ACKNOWLEDGEMENTS

Several pieces have been previously published and I thank the editors for selecting my work. They are listed in the order of appearance.

"Cilantro," *Anti-Heroin Chic*, August 2022.
"Tomato Harvest Management," *Bird Seed Magazine* Vol. I issue 2.
"Sunflowers," *Dribble Drabble Review*, Vol. V, Anthology 1, 2022
"Admiration for My Grandmother's Pitcher," *Open Journal of Arts and Letters*, January 2022.
"The Nature of Basil," *Miniskirt Magazine* Vol. I issue 9, 2021.
"Red Tomato Harvest" and "Recipe for Fried Tofu," *The Inquisitive Eater*, April 2024.
"Fall Garden" and "Gardeners Call Them Volunteers," *Meat for Tea*, Vol. 17, Issue 3, Casserole, 2023.
"Love in the Kitchen," *Pareidolia Literary*, Vol. 2. Wunderkammer, 2021.
"The Simple Joys of Baking Cake," *Random Sample Review*, Issue 7, Summer 2022.
"Menudo," *Full House Literary*, Featured Creator January 2022.
"We Bought the Kelly Green Dress," *Lumiere Review*, Party Time issue, 2021. "At Age Eight We Were Young Enough to Trespass," *Across the Margin*, May 2023.
"Voice Lessons," *Litro Magazine*, July 30. 2022.
"Freedom," *Sledgehammer Literary Journal*, 2021.
"The Land Holds My Memory," *Invisible City Literary Magazine*, Issue 3, Fall 2021.
"Bareback Rider" *Thin Air Magazine*, Vol. 27, 2021.
"The Story of the Family Samovar," *Lunch Ticket*, Fall 2020 and *Sugar, Sugar Salt*, December 2023.
"Back to School Night," *Stonecoast Review*, Issue No. 19, Summer 2023.
"Lost and Found," *Across the Margin*, May 2023.

Many people have helped me on my writing journey. Thank you to my dear friend and teacher Lynn Schwartz, who introduced me to flash prose, and to writer colleague Jane Elkin, who inspired me to pursue an MFA and who, along with Vicki Meade, were my weekly workshop partners during Covid. Valuable feedback on many of the pieces in this volume came from writers: Sandy Collier, Stephanie Loleng, Linda Mahal, and Leah Siviski.

Acknowledgements

From my first semester workshop with Indigo Moor to my final semester workshop on publishing with Suzanne Strempek Shea, my participation in the low-residency MFA Stonecoast Writing Program at the University of Southern Maine was transformative. A special thanks to my four mentors, Cara Hoffman, Elizabeth Searle, Aaron Hamburger, and Susan Conley. I think about you often.

Thank you also to my husband Peter, my brother David, and my children, Justin, Christopher, Alex, and their respective families that include so many wonderful grandchildren.

And last but not least, I would like to thank Dianne Pearce, who invited me to join the Old Scratch Short Form Collective. Dianne had a dream she wanted to publish a series of poetry chapbooks if a collective of writers could help organize, edit, and publicize the books. And it happened. Eleven of us have been working together; several books have been published, and I am number five. Thank you also to Co-publisher David Yurkovich for your technical and design talents, enabling this volume to come to fruition, and to fellow authors, Alan Bern, Gabby Gilliam and Morgan Golladay for proofreading and feedback.

ABOUT THE AUTHOR

Nadja Maril's poems, essays, short stories, and novel excerpts have been published in *The Lumiere Review, Lunch Ticket, Spry Literary Journal, Change Seven, Litro Magazine, Zin Daily, BarBar, The Sunlight Press* and other publications. She  grew up in Baltimore and wrote and directed her first play at age seven. Nadja earned an MFA in Creative Writing from the Stonecoast Program at the University of Southern Maine and is a Contributing Editor for Old Scratch Press. She lives in Annapolis, Maryland.

A former freelance journalist, weekly columnist and editor, her articles have appeared in such magazines and newspapers as: *Victorian Homes, Chesapeake Taste, Old House Journal, The Cape Cod Times, The Annapolis Capital, What's Up? Media,* and *The Washington Post.* She is also the author of two reference books, *American Lighting 1840-1940* and *Antique Lamp Buyer's Guide.*

Nadja Maril's children's books—*Me, Molly Midnight: the Artist's Cat,* and *Runaway Molly Midnight: the Artist's Cat* —were collaborative projects with her father, artist Herman Maril, whose paintings and drawings illustrate the stories that are set in one of her favorite places—Cape Cod. Nadja is also the author and illustrator of *Who is Santa?* a book for all ages.

An inveterate blogger, Nadja's weekly musings often include writing prompts and original recipes.

More at nadjamaril.com.

Who IS Santa?

Poem & Pictures by NADJA MARIL

Who IS Santa?

By Nadja Maril

Who is Santa?, a children's picture book by writer/poet Nadja Maril, tackles the mystery of Santa Claus and conveys the spirit of giving in a delightful story both youngsters and adults will enjoy.

"In *Who is Santa?* Nadja Maril tackles the difficult and perennial question kids have about Santa: How can one Santa be everywhere giving presents to everyone? Maril answers the question with her straight-ahead words and her entirely delightful illustrations to reassure kids about Santa and even include them in Santa's ever-present generosity."
Alan Bern, author, *In the Pace of the Path*, and retired children's librarian

"A clever and meaningful interpretation of Santa with a message that's just as important for the grownups as it is for the kids. Plan to make this book an annual Christmas tradition for your family."
Dylan Roche, author of *The Purple Bird* and *The Tide and the Stars*

All proceeds from the sale of this book will be donated to the International Pleuropulmonary Blastoma (PPB)/DICER1 Registry. The mission of the registry is to improve outcomes for children and adults with pleuropulmonary blastoma (PPB) and other DICER1-related cancers.

8.5 x 8.5 paperback with full color cover and interiors | $11.95 US

Available at Amazon and better bookstores.

break in the field

ELLIS ELLIOTT

Break in the Field

By Ellis Elliott

Break in the Field by Ellis Elliott is a captivating and heartfelt poetry collection. Deeply personal, Ellis' collection looks at the enlightening experience of parenting a profoundly disabled stepson, while simultaneously embracing the other shifts in mid-life.

A 2023 National Book Award nominee title, this outstanding collection is a work you'll want to revisit time and again.

"A deeply felt collection of candid verse."
KIRKUS

"Ellis Elliott's compelling *Break in the Field* creates associations between humanity, nature, and time that deserve not only individual inspection and appreciation, but spirited discussions about contemporary poetry's ability to attract and react to life's events with bigger-picture reflections about growth, freedom, and life lessons."
Midwest Book Review

"This gripping, heart wrenching exploration of her inner most thoughts and feelings while caring for her extreme needs stepson, "[whose] brain vessels shattered at birth into a million stars," are so raw, so deeply forthright, from a place of such compassion, tenderness, and introspection that I found myself tearful many times."
Kari Gunter Seymour
Ohio Poet Laureate and author of
Alone in the House of My Heart

6 x 9 paperback with color covers | $9.99 US

Available at Amazon and better bookstores.

white noir

robert fleming

white noir

By Robert Fleming

Old Scratch Press proudly unveils the sensational collection by avant-garde wordsmith and visual artist, Robert Fleming, as we introduce *white noir*.

Where Art Meets Poetry: Fleming's creative prowess knows no bounds. He's a poet who wields images like a maestro conducts a symphony, infusing each verse with a visual narrative that ignites the imagination. Brace yourself for an electrifying literary experience that shatters the boundaries of storytelling.

A Feast for the Mind and the Eyes: *white noir* is more than poetry; it's a a tapestry of emotions on paper. Featuring a striking cover designed by the author. It's not just a book; it's an artistic revelation! "You will see and think things you never did," says **Matt Wall,** publisher of Poetic Anarchy Press, while **Michael Sindler**, beat poet laureate of Colorado, "Robert Fleming is outrageous and original in word and image."

...the tempo, emotional connections, rich and unexpected overlays of subject, and excitingly thought-provoking approaches to poetry deserve wider appreciation than the typical contemporary poetic presentation. **Midwest Book Review**

"...a raw and curious visual journey through human history."
Crystal Heidel
Author, *Still Life in Blood* and owner of Byzantium Sky Press

6 x 9 paperback with black and white cover and interiors | $8.99 US

Available at Amazon and better bookstores.

The Song of North Mountain

Morgan Golladay

The Song of North Mountain

By Morgan Golladay

From the mighty pen of artist and author Morgan Golladay comes *The Song of North Mountain*, a transformative collection of poetry and art celebrating the famous and mystical North Mountain of Appalachia.

North Mountain, a wildland in the George Washington and Jefferson National Forests of western Virginia, has been recognized by the Wilderness Society as a special place worthy of protection from logging and road construction. The Wilderness Society has designated the area as a "Mountain Treasure." Morgan Golladay brings her readers to dwell in the reverence of this wonderful wilderness.

Golladay is an award-winning author and illustrator who was raised on North Mountain and lives in coastal Delaware as part of a thriving artist and author community.

The Song of North Mountain is National Book Award nominee!

"Sometimes stark, but always beautiful, these free verse celebrations of North Mountain introduce a seasonal sense of environmental transitions to the observer and reader's eye, with time's passage changing everything and nothing...Aside from a personal visit to North Mountain, there is no better way of appreciating its beauty, impact, and presence over the eons than through *The Song of North Mountain*."
Midwest Book Review

6 x 9 paperback with full color and B&W interior art | $9.99 US

Available at Amazon and better bookstores.

No Ocean
Spit Me Out

Gabby Gilliam

No Ocean Spit Me Out

By Gabby Gilliam

No Ocean Spit Me Out is a captivating debut collection of poetry by Gabby Gilliam that delves deep into the intricate tapestry of family dynamics and personal evolution. Within its 30 poems, the collection embarks on a profound journey through the stages of coming of age, navigating the complexities of familial bonds, grappling with organized religion, and ultimately, embracing the essence of self-acceptance. Each poem in this collection serves as a poignant reflection of the human experience, capturing moments of vulnerability, resilience, and growth with eloquence. Through lyrical prose and emotive imagery, Gilliam paints a vivid portrait of the joys and struggles inherent in the process of self-discovery.

Whether you're seeking solace in the shared experiences of family relationships or searching for introspective insights into the nuances of identity and faith, Gilliam's collection offers a profound and thought-provoking exploration of the human condition.

Gabby Gilliam's verse preserves the feel of the summer farm, contrasting its fertile brightness with the struggle between grief and the sudden absence of connection to family and place.
Kim Malinowski
Author, *Home*

No Ocean Spit Me Out is filled with warm memories of time spent in Upstate New York with her grandparents. In her poems, she revisits the farm and the people she loves as a child, an adolescent and an adult. The reader is invited into this loving world.
Lynne Kemen
Author, *Shoes for Lucy*

6 x 9 paperback with full color and B&W interior art | $9.99 US

Available at Amazon and better bookstores.

Λ page turner. Your story. In print.

Learn more at currentwords.com.

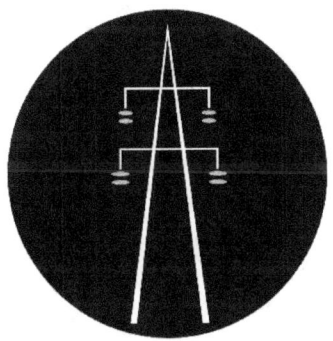

Introducing Current Words

We're a full-service partner publisher ready to help you complete your personal and professional writing goals. Whether you're seeking an entire publishing package that includes editing, book design, book trailer, and published book and eBook or individual services, we have the experience to help guarantee your total satisfaction. Why clients choose us...

PERSONAL ENGAGEMENT
We prioritize forming genuine connections with our clients.

40+ YEARS OF COMBINED EXPERIENCE
Our team brings decades of expertise to every project.

ATTENTIVENESS TO YOUR NEEDS
Your vision is our priority, and we tailor our services to meet your unique requirements.

TOP-QUALITY EDITING, PRODUCTION, AND DESIGN
We maintain the highest standards to ensure your manuscript shines.

HONESTY AND INTEGRITY
Trust is the foundation of our relationship with clients, and we uphold it with transparent communication and ethical practices.

With Current Words, your manuscript will receive the world- class treatment it deserves. Dive into our website today and discover how we can help you achieve your publishing goals!

currentwords.com

Old Scratch Press

Founded in 2023, Old Scratch Press is a cooperative of poets and short-form authors who have come together to promote the publication and appreciation of poetry and short-form writing. The Press exists on 100% volunteer labor.

It is financially supported by Current Words Publishing and features multiple opportunities for publication. There is no charge to submit or publish work with Old Scratch Press.

To learn more visit oldscratchpress.com.

www.ingramcontent.com/pod-product-compliance
Lightning Source LLC
Chambersburg PA
CBHW051009140626
46546CB00016B/1374